WHO AM I
TO JUDGE?

T0364051

Running Press
Hachette Book Group
1290 Avenue of the Americas, New York, NY 10104
www.runningpress.com
@Running_Press

First Edition: April 2015

Published by Running Press, an imprint of Perseus Books, LLC,
a subsidiary of Hachette Book Group, Inc. The Running Press
name and logo is a trademark of the Hachette Book Group.

The Hachette Speakers Bureau provides a wide range
of authors for speaking events. To find out more, go to
www.hachettespeakersbureau.com or call (866) 376-6591.

The publisher is not responsible for websites (or their content)
that are not owned by the publisher.

ISBN: 978-0-7624-5692-5

INTRODUCTION

*P*OPE FRANCIS, THE 266TH SUPREME Pontiff, was born Jorge Mario Bergoglio in Buenos Aires, Argentina. He became the Archbishop of Buenos Aires in 1998 and was named a cardinal by Pope John Paul II in 2001. He is the first non-European pontiff in 1,300 years.

He chose his title to honor Francis of Assisi, patron saint of the environment and an advocate for the impoverished. This intentional choice reflects Pope Francis's core beliefs: He is a champion of environmental protection, rallies against consumerism, and believes the church should eliminate poverty through direct pastoral work. Known for his less formal approach to the papacy, Pope Francis chooses to reside in a Vatican guesthouse and regularly ministers directly to the poor and sick.

In his first years as Pope, Pope Francis has shared his outlook through letters, apostolic exhortations, radio and video addresses, and often unscripted speeches directly to the people. Presented here is a collection of some of Pope Francis's most well-known quotes to reflect his unique voice.

"I prefer a Church which is bruised, hurting, and dirty because it has been out on the streets, rather than a Church which is unhealthy from being confined and from clinging to its own security."

(Apostolic exhortation "Evangelii Gaudium," November, 2013)

"If one has the answers to all the questions—that is the proof that God is not with him. It means that he is a false prophet using religion for himself. The great leaders of the people of God, like Moses, have always left room for doubt."

(America magazine, September, 2013)

"Men and women are sacrificed to the idols of profit and consumption: It is the 'culture of waste.' If you break a computer it is a tragedy, but poverty, the needs, the dramas of so many people end up becoming the norm."

(Vatican Radio, June, 2013)

"I see the church as a field hospital after battle. It is useless to ask a seriously injured person if he has high cholesterol and about the level of his blood sugars! You have to heal his wounds. Then we can talk about everything else."

(America magazine, September, 2013)

"I am thinking of what Saint Ignatius told us . . . he pointed out two criteria on love. The first: Love is expressed more clearly in actions than in words. The second: There is greater love in giving than in receiving."

(Morning Meditation in the chapel of the Domus Sanctæ Marthæ, June, 2013)

"Violence and war lead only to death, they speak of death! Violence and war are the language of death!"

(Vigil of Prayer for Peace in Saint Peter's Square, September, 2013)

"We are in front of a global scandal of around one billion people who still suffer from hunger today. We cannot look the other way and pretend this does not exist. The food available in the world is enough to feed everyone."

(In a video message launching "One Human Family, Food For All," a global campaign against hunger, December, 2013)

"Faith is not a light which scatters all our darkness, but a lamp which guides our steps in the night and suffices for the journey."

(Lumen fidei, *Encyclical Letter of Pope Francis co-written with Pope Emeritus Benedict XVI, June, 2013*)

"It is so terrible to gossip! At first it may seem like a nice thing, even amusing, like enjoying a candy. But in the end, it fills the heart with bitterness, and even poisons us."

(Angelus in Saint Peter's Square, February, 2014)

"Although the life of a person
is a land full of thorns and weeds,
there is always a space in
which the good seed can grow.
You have to trust God."

(Interview in the New York Times,
September, 2013)

"We all have the duty
to do good."

(Vatican Radio, May, 2013)

"Worshipping is stripping ourselves of our idols, even the most hidden ones, and choosing the Lord as the center, as the highway of our lives."

(Eucharistic Celebration in Basilica of Saint Paul Outside-the-Walls, April, 2013)

This book has been bound using handcraft methods and Smyth-sewn to ensure durability.

The cover and interior were designed by Frances J. Soo Ping Chow.

The introduction was written by and quotes compiled by Danielle Selber.

The text was edited by Jordana Tusman.

The text was set in Baskerville and Trade Gothic.